my first
CAMPING
BOOK

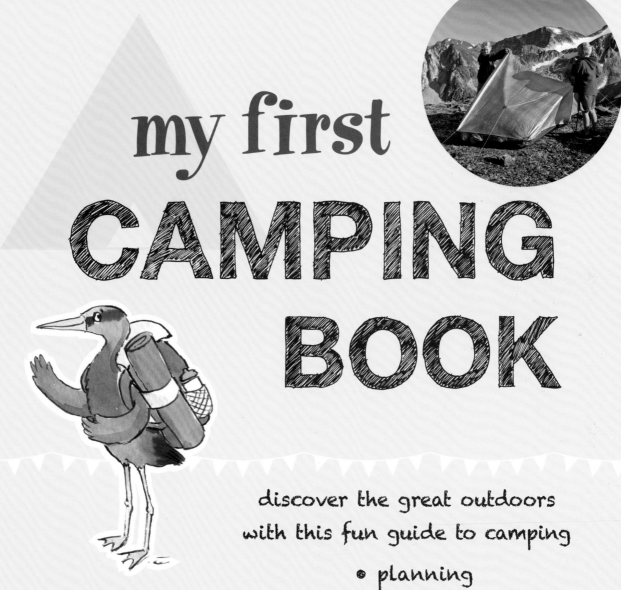

my first CAMPING BOOK

discover the great outdoors
with this fun guide to camping

- planning
- cooking
- safety
- activities

Dominic Bliss

CICO **kidz**

For Daisy and Lola Bliss, who always hog all the space in the tent.

Published in 2015 by CICO Books

An imprint of Ryland Peters & Small Ltd
20–21 Jockey's Fields, London WC1R 4BW
341 E 116th St, New York, NY 10029

www.rylandpeters.com

10 9 8 7 6 5 4 3 2

Text © Dominic Bliss 2015
Design and illustration © CICO Books 2015
Photography © Corbis Images 2015, except pages 6
(top right), 29, 36, 38, 42, 44, 83, 85, 87, and 89
© CICO Books 2015

A CIP catalog record for this book is available from the Library of Congress and the British Library.

ISBN: 978 1 78249 198 9

Printed in China

Editor: Rosie Lewis
Series consultant: Susan Akass
Designer: Rosamund Saunders
Illustrator: Rachel Boulton
Character illustrations: Hannah George

In-house editor: Anna Galkina
In-house designer: Fahema Khanam
Art director: Sally Powell
Production controller: Meskerem Berhane
Publishing manager: Penny Craig
Publisher: Cindy Richards

The author and the publishers cannot accept any legal responsibility for any personal injury to children arising from the advice and activities outlined in this book. Every care has been taken to provide safety advice where needed.

Contents

Introduction

Are you ready for a great big adventure in the countryside? Camping is great fun whether you're a grown-up or a kid . . . but especially if you're a kid.

There's so much to do—building fires, wild swimming, hiking, tracking animals, sleeping-bag races, telling ghost stories, stargazing. All your friends will wish they could come too!

In *My First Camping Book* there are four chapters. First, Get Ready to Camp tells you how and where to put up a tent properly, how to decorate your tent so it's the best-looking one on the campsite, and all the things you need to bring to guarantee that you have a really good time.

Chapter Two, Campsite Cooking, is all about fire—how to build and light a fire safely (you'll need a grown-up to help you with this), and how to cook some (hopefully) delicious meals. There are also some great camping recipes, sure to get your tummy really rumbling.

In Chapter Three, Camping Activities, you'll find loads of ideas for cool things to do on your trip: treasure trails, tree-climbing, animal-spotting, pond-dipping, sleeping-bag races. You'll be jumping out of your sleeping bag and scrambling from your tent to get started on these.

Finally, in Chapter Four, When the Sun Goes Down, you'll discover all the campsite activities you can do after dark. What about catching some moths? Or making shadow puppets in your tent? Or stargazing—use our guide to see what you can see in the night sky. And no camping trip is complete without telling scary ghost stories before you go to sleep.

chapter 1
Get Ready to Camp

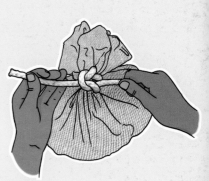

What to take with you

When you go camping with family or friends, the grown-ups will pack most of the stuff you need, such as tents, sleeping bags, and cooking equipment. What you should do is pack your own backpack with the extra bits and pieces of equipment that will make your trip really fun and exciting. So, before you head off on your trip, check you have everything you need.

Flashlight (torch): Remember that there are no streetlights outside towns. Without a flashlight you won't see a thing once the sun goes down. You definitely need one of your own for exploring in the dark, or for when you wake up in the night. It's also a good idea to bring spare batteries, just in case.

Magnifying glass or bug pot (a transparent pot with a magnifying lid) for examining all the strange and fascinating bugs you might encounter in the wild.

Binoculars: Great for bird-spotting and stargazing.

Pencil case with pencils, colored pencils, colored pens, and a gold or silver pen for filling in your diary, making maps and pendants, or having fun when it's raining outside. Also bring scissors, string, a glue stick, paints, and plain paper for making other stuff!

Compass: Essential if you go hiking.

Camera: Be sure to keep it in a very solid case, and then wrap the case in a plastic bag so it doesn't get wet.

Wildlife books: When you're camping in the countryside, internet access is always very patchy. Take wildlife books with you so you can identify cool animals and plants.

Book or printouts of ghost stories: Perfect for spooky campfire tales.

Water bottle: You will need to drink plenty when you're out and about.

Hat, sunscreen, and sunglasses: You're going to be outside all day, so protect yourself from the sun.

Penknife: Great for opening cans, cutting up food, and whittling wood. Get permission from a grown-up before you use one, though.

Wooly hat: For when the sun goes down and it begins to get cold. You can even wear it in bed!

Teddy bear (or other favorite soft toy): For when you wake up in the night and hear strange noises outside the tent!

Keeping a camp diary

In years to come you'll want to remember your first camping trips. As well as taking photos, it's a great idea to keep a camp diary, too. In it you can note down where you went camping, what games you played and activities you did, what camping skills you learned, which cool animals and plants you spotted, and what you cooked on the campfire. But don't just buy a diary at the stationery store—it's much better to make your own.

You will need:

Lots of sheets of paper (colored paper looks better than plain white)

Two sheets of cardboard (from an old carton)

Sticky tape

Pencil

Ruler

Scissors

Hole punch

Thick string

Glue stick

Envelope

Pen

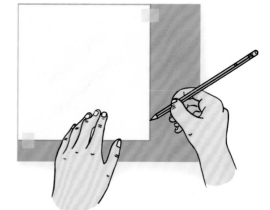

1 Stick one piece of paper to the cardboard with a piece of sticky tape, then carefully draw around it using the pencil and ruler. Cut it out carefully and then draw round it onto the other piece of cardboard. Cut that out too. The cardboard will be your diary cover, the sheets of paper your diary pages. Ask a grown-up to help you cut the cardboard if it's really thick.

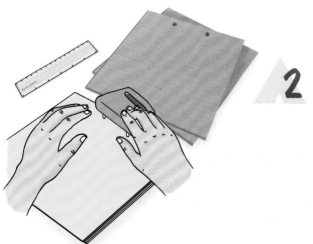

2 Using the hole punch, make holes on one edge of both pieces of the cardboard and the sheets of paper. If you have lots of paper, the sheets may not fit into the hole punch all at once, so you'll have to separate them into several piles. Use the ruler to make sure you punch holes through each pile in the same place.

Place all the sheets of paper in between the two pieces of cardboard (like a sandwich) and line up all the holes.

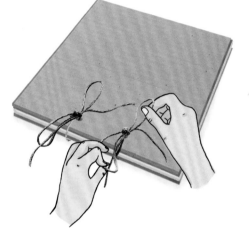

 Using the glue stick, spread glue over the front of the envelope (where you'd normally write the address) and stick it neatly to the inside of the front cover of your diary. You can use this envelope to collect leaves and seeds you find when you're camping.

Thread a piece of string through each hole and tie it with a bow—not too tight, though, or you won't be able to turn the pages.

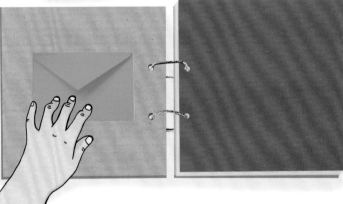

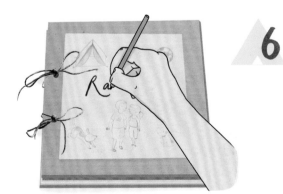

Glue a piece of colored paper to the front of your diary. (The paper should be slightly smaller than the cover.) Write your name on it in the middle and decorate the edge with camping drawings: maybe a tent and a campfire, plus some plants and animals you expect to see.

How to put up your tent

No two tents are exactly the same: some just pop up on their own or can be inflated with a pump, while some big ones can be quite tricky to put up. However, they are all much easier to cope with if you and the rest of your camping group work as a team and have your own jobs to do. Follow any instructions that come with the tent and get used to the way it all works. If you can, practice pitching your tent in your yard (garden) before you head off on your camping trip.

Here are some tips for putting up your tent successfully:

1 Lay out all the tent materials and equipment neatly on the ground. Make sure all the zippers are done up. If you have a separate groundsheet, lay it down on the spot you've chosen for your tent. (See Where to pitch your tent, page 18.)

2 If there are tent poles, connect them together—modern ones usually have elastic shock cords to link them up. Find out where the poles have to go and gently slide them through the sleeves. Don't force the poles or you might rip the tent fabric. On most tents the poles will slot into rings or cups at the bottom corners.

3

It's time to bang in some tent pegs. With some tents the groundsheet is separate, but with many it is attached to the inner tent. However yours is made, you will need to stretch out all four corners so that it is nice and flat with no wrinkles. Use a mallet or a rock to hammer the pegs through the rings in the corners of the groundsheet into the ground. Hammer the pegs at an angle with the top end pointing away from the tent, so that the rings can't come loose.

4

Some tents have a single layer, while some have an inner tent that hangs from an outer one, and some have an outer layer that is put up over the inner one. Whichever type you have, remember: the outer shell mustn't touch the inner tent or water might leak through during the night.

5 Whatever type of tent you have, you will now have to hammer in some more tent pegs through the loop and rings around your tent, remembering to stretch out the corners of your tent. Finally, stretch out the guy ropes and peg them into the ground. Get them nice and tight so that the tent doesn't flap. Make sure the guy ropes don't block access to the tent door.

Key:

1 Entrance
2 Poles
3 Groundsheet
4 Inner tent
5 Tent pegs
6 Guy ropes
7 Outer shell (or flysheet)

Where to pitch your tent

Whether you're camping right out in the wilderness or in a very safe campsite, there are important things you must remember before you pitch your tent.

1 Always pitch your tent before the sun goes down, otherwise you'll be stumbling around in the dark looking for tent pegs. You'll be surprised just how dark it gets in the countryside.

2 Choose a flat, dry section of ground, with no sharp stones or thorns. Even with a thick groundsheet under your tent, these can be very uncomfortable once you lie down inside.

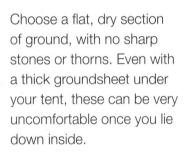

If you have to pitch your tent on sloping ground, make sure you lie with your feet pointing downhill.

 A sheltered spot is nice, but avoid a pitch beneath a tree where birds like roosting. Otherwise you may find your tent gets redecorated!

5 Avoid a pitch that might get waterlogged if it rains. Ditches, dips in the ground, and places very near lakes and rivers can all flood if there's heavy rain overnight, so check the weather before you go. Still water also attracts nasty biting insects in the summer.

6 Think about which way the wind is blowing. A sheltered spot will stop the tent from flapping all night in the breeze. On a cold night you want the tent entrance to face away from the wind, so that cold air doesn't blow in. On a very warm night you'll need a breeze to keep you cool.

7 Think about where the sun will shine in the early morning. It can get as hot as a sauna inside a tent once the sun rises. Remember—the sun rises in the east and sets in the west.

8 If you're in a campsite, don't pitch too close to the bathrooms. You'll get woken very early in the morning, and it can be a bit smelly!

Nature's nasties

In some parts of the world you must watch out for dangerous animals and poisonous plants. It all depends on where you're camping and in which country. A few basic rules will keep you safe, though:

- Always wear socks and boots when hiking through thick undergrowth.
- Avoid putting your hands inside holes and under logs when you can't see what's there.
- Ask a grown-up which dangerous plants and animals to look out for.
- Always check inside boots or shoes before you put them on, as these make great hiding-places for creepy-crawlies.

An animal-proof larder

It won't take long for ants, bugs and wild animals to sniff out all your lovely food. To stop them getting to it, you need a larder you can hang up high in a tree.

You will need:

Small plate

Large drawstring muslin bag (very cheap from a kitchen store)

Rope

Yes, you can buy a fabric hanging larder with proper hooks and zippers from a camping store. But you can also make your own much more basic version.

1 Place the small plate in the bottom of the muslin bag with your food on top of it. (The food must still be wrapped up inside a plastic bag.) Remember that a hanging larder will not keep food cold in the way a refrigerator would, so it isn't suitable for meat, fish or other food that will go bad.

2 Close the muslin bag and tie one end of the rope tightly around the opening.

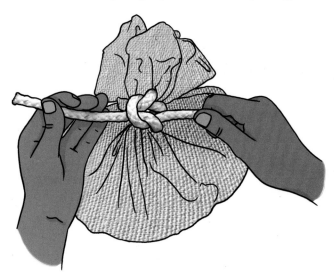

 3 Ask a grown-up to stretch the rope over a high branch that's well shaded and tie the other end of the rope around the trunk of the tree.

 4 You can let the hanging larder down when you need to get food out of it, and you can pull it back up whenever you leave camp.

SAFETY FIRST

If you are camping in a place where there are likely to be bears, this hanging larder will not be suitable, as bears can climb trees! You will need to keep all your food in your car, in the metal container that is provided by some campsites, or you can buy a bear-proof food canister in a camping store.

Decorating your tent

In a busy campsite you'll never forget where your tent is if you decorate it with bunting. Even out in the countryside it's fun to make your tent more colorful. Make some decorations at home ready for your camping trip.

Bunting

With lots of little flags flapping in the breeze, bunting can look really cool, especially if you string it up between two tents.

You will need:

....

Scraps of different-colored fabric

Sharp scissors

Paper, pencil, and ruler

String

Craft (PVA) glue

Dressmaking pins

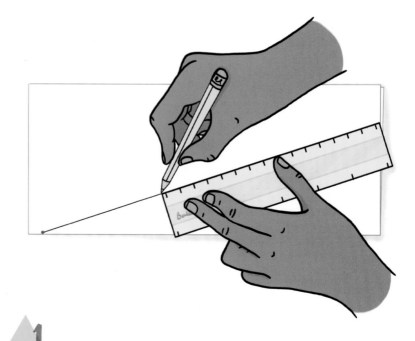

1 Make a template for cutting out the flags. To do this, fold a sheet of paper in half. Measure 9 in. (23 cm) up the crease from the bottom and make a dot with your pencil. Measure 3 in. (7.5 cm) from the crease and make another dot. Join the two dots with the ruler. Cut along this line to make a triangle and then open it out to make a bigger triangle.

2 Pin the template to a piece of fabric and cut around it with sharp scissors. Cut out lots of triangles in the same way.

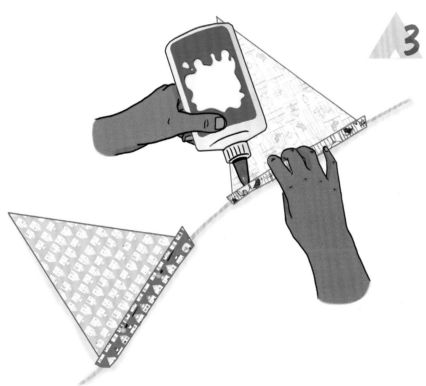

3 Taking one flag at a time, smear glue along the top edge of the flag and fold it carefully over the string. Hold each one in place until it dries, and then cut off the little triangle flaps made by your fold. (Be careful not to cut the string!) If the glue is taking a long time to dry, you could use pins to hold the fabric while you move on to the next flags. The flags should be glued just a couple inches (about 5 cm) apart along the string.

Guy-rope bunting

Stick brightly colored or reflective tape around the guy ropes. It looks great and should stop you (or anyone else) from tripping over them.

Tent flags

You can buy telescopic flag poles in a camping store. To make a flag, cut a piece of fabric (the more colorful the better, but an old T-shirt will do) into a rectangular shape and fold it around the flag pole, sticking it tight with glue. Now place your sapling in the ground near your tent so that it waves in the wind.

chapter 2
Campsite Cooking

How to make a campfire 30

Great campfire recipes 36

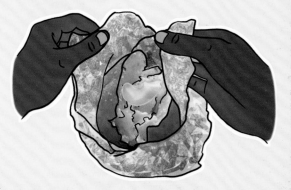

How to make a campfire

One of the highlights of a camping trip is to build a campfire and sit around the crackling flames as you tell stories and toast marshmallows. However, before you build a fire, make sure that it is allowed on your site and that there are no fire bans in force (see box on page 31).

1 Choose a flat patch of bare ground away from tents, trees, and overhanging branches. Make a circle of rocks a few feet across to surround your fire. Have some water ready just in case a stray spark blows onto your tent and sets it alight.

2 Scout around your camp for lots of dry, dead wood. You'll need twigs and sticks of all sizes, from very tiny ones (called kindling) up to small logs. Once you've collected the wood, split it into different piles according to size. If it's been raining recently you may have to search under large logs or rocks, or beneath trees, to find dry wood.

3 Now you need tinder—that's the name of the material you start your fire with. If the weather has been very dry you can use dead leaves, moss, dried grass, lichen, or thin, dead bark. If the weather's a bit damp you may need paper.

4 Place the tinder at the base of the fire with the tiniest twigs on top. Make sure there's lots of space for air to flow in. Now, using slightly bigger twigs, build a pyramid around the tinder.

5 Light the base of your fire with a match or cigarette lighter. It's very important that a grown-up supervises you at this point. Have your back to the wind so that the flame blows away from you, and, if you are striking a match, make sure to strike it away from you. Gently blow on the fire to encourage it. Be careful not to get your face or head too close.

You are not allowed to build fires just anywhere, whenever you want. Depending on which country you live in, you may be able to build fires when wilderness camping, but in the UK this is not allowed without the landowner's permission. Many campsites do not allow fires close to tents, but some allow you to light fires in specially built fire pits. (Check this out when you book your site.) Alternatively, you may be able to camp on a friend's land, and then you can ask their permission to build a fire. Or you could even camp in your own backyard (garden) and choose a special place for your fire. Remember, though, that before you build a fire you should find out about any fire bans in your area. Fire bans usually come into force when the weather has been hot and dry for a long time and there is a big danger of bush fires.

FIRE SAFETY

If you light a campfire you must remember some safety rules:

• Never run around the fire.

• Never take a burning stick from the fire.

• Never throw anything onto the fire—ask an adult to help you to put wood on carefully (otherwise sparks could fly out).

• Do not sit down-wind of a fire or the smoke will blow into your eyes. If the wind changes and blows smoke in your direction, turn your face to one side, put your hand over your face, and close your eyes while you count to thirty.

 6 As your fire gets stronger, you can gradually add larger and larger sticks to it. Make sure you always leave space for the air to flow in, though. Eventually your fire will be so strong that you can place small logs on top.

7 Never leave the fire unattended. When it has burned out, douse it with water to make sure it doesn't·catch light again while you're asleep.

Cooking on a campfire

If you want to cook on your campfire, you'll need to rest your pots and pans above the flames. The best way to do this is to build a log-cabin shape around your pyramid fire.

1 Gather lots of long, thick logs, all about the same length. Use green wood, because you don't want these logs to burn.

2 Use the logs to make a square log-cabin shape. There should be enough room inside the log cabin to make a normal pyramid-shape fire (see page 31). Overlap the ends of the logs so that the four walls fit together and don't roll around. There should be gaps between the logs so that air can move through your fire.

If you don't want to bother with pots and pans, you can cook some foods by holding them directly over the fire on the end of a long-handled toasting/barbecue fork, or a long, thin, green stick that you have chosen specially. (The sticks and handles need to be long so that your hand doesn't get too close to the fire.) Marshmallows, hot dogs, apples, pineapple, zucchini (courgette), and squash are perfect for this. If you don't want to burn them, remember to wait until the flames have died down and the embers are still glowing. Spread a bit of olive oil on the vegetables and butter on the fruit, to stop them from getting charred. Be really careful not to burn your fingers.

The other way to cook food is by wrapping it in foil and placing it on the hot coals of your fire. Wait until the flames have died down a bit, and use long-handled tongs to take the food out of the fire when it's cooked, otherwise you'll burn your fingers. Always ask an adult to help you when putting anything into the fire, taking it out, or turning it over.

Of course, you may be using an outdoor grill rather than a campfire, it's a lot easier and quicker to make your meals this way, but not as fun!

Great campfire recipes

When you're out in the country, camping—with no oven, no microwave, no refrigerator, and no sink—you need recipes that are quick and easy to make.

Jacket potatoes

Corn on the cob

Hot dogs

Baked apples

S'mores

Jacket potatoes

It will take almost an hour to cook big potatoes in their jackets on a campfire, so get them started early if you can. The crispy skins and fluffy insides—which you'll spread with lots of butter—are well worth the wait.

Ingredients:

Medium-size baking potatoes

Olive oil

Butter

Sea salt and black pepper

1 Scrub each potato clean and rub a little olive oil into the skin.

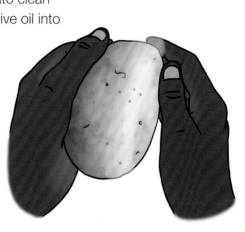

2 Using a fork, pierce the potatoes all over—this will stop them from exploding in the fire!

3 Wrap each potato (one per person will be enough) in a double layer of foil.

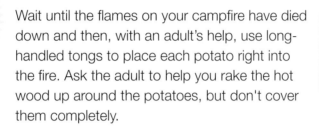

4 Wait until the flames on your campfire have died down and then, with an adult's help, use long-handled tongs to place each potato right into the fire. Ask the adult to help you rake the hot wood up around the potatoes, but don't cover them completely.

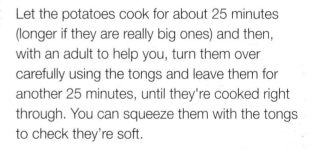

5 Let the potatoes cook for about 25 minutes (longer if they are really big ones) and then, with an adult to help you, turn them over carefully using the tongs and leave them for another 25 minutes, until they're cooked right through. You can squeeze them with the tongs to check they're soft.

6 Again with an adult's help, use the tongs to take the potatoes out of the fire and let them cool for a few minutes.

7 After checking the foil isn't too hot, carefully unwrap the potatoes and cut them in half. Mash the insides a little with a fork. Put a small piece of butter and a sprinkle of salt and pepper on each one, and hand them round.

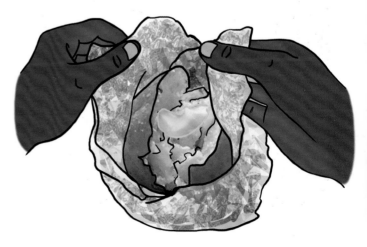

Corn on the cob

Yes, you'll be picking bits of corn from your teeth for ages afterward, but that's alright because you're in a campsite. You don't need perfect table manners.

Ingredients:

Cobs of corn with the husks still on

Butter

Herbs, such as thyme (optional)

Salt and pepper

1 Soak the corn cobs in cool, clean water for about an hour before you cook them. This stops the husks from burning when you put them on the campfire.

2 When the flames have died down a bit, ask an adult to help you place the cobs on the hot coals using long-handled tongs.

3 Cook the cobs for 15 minutes, using the tongs to turn them regularly with an adult's help. The husks will be charred all over.

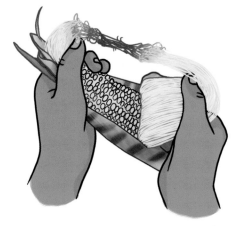

4 Take the cobs off the fire and let them cool, then carefully peel off the husks.

5 Now, push a long-handled metal toasting/barbecue fork into one end and grill the open cobs for a few minutes by holding them over the fire and turning them slowly. The corn kernels will turn brown.

6 Put the cobs on a plate and spread butter over them while they're still hot. Add the herbs (if you have some), salt, and pepper. Get munching!

Hot dogs

Hot dogs cooked over the fire are a camping tradition. Go for pre-cooked frankfurters so you don't have to worry about under-cooking your sausages by mistake. You can buy them in cans and jars, which is really useful for camping as they don't need to be kept in a fridge.

Ingredients:

Pre-cooked frankfurters

Hot-dog buns

Sliced tomatoes

Ketchup, barbecue sauce, mustard, and black pepper

1 A two-pronged, long-handled toasting fork is the best tool for hot dogs, as it holds them more securely than a single stick. Push a hot dog onto the fork (you might be able to fit on two or three at a time!) and heat it for a few minutes over the campfire, turning it all the time until it is hot. Don't worry about under-cooking it, since these are pre-cooked ones. Put it onto a metal plate close to the fire to keep warm while you cook the next one.

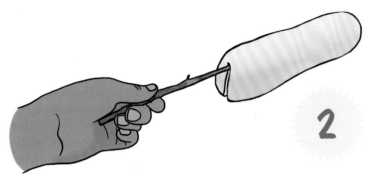

2 While you are cooking the sausages get someone else to slit the bun down the middle, but leave it in one piece. Your helper should then toast it over the fire using a toasting fork (or a stick if you only have one fork).

3 When everything is ready, slap a hot sausage in each bun, along with some slices of tomato.

4 Hand the hot dogs around, and tell your fellow campers to add their own relishes. Maybe go easy on the mustard!

Baked apples

This is a healthy campfire dessert. The apple gets
really gooey inside and tastes delicious.

Ingredients:

For each person you will need:

1 apple

1 tsp brown sugar

½ tsp cinnamon

1 tbsp dried fruit, such as raisins or sultanas
(optional)

1 tsp butter

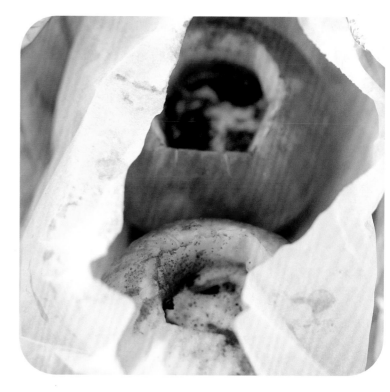

2 Mix the brown sugar and
cinnamon in a bowl.

1 Ask a grown-up to cut
out the core of the apples
without cutting right
through the bottom. If
you do cut right through,
push a short plug of
apple back into the hole.

3 If you are using dried fruit, spoon
this into the hole in the apple and
push it down firmly.

4 Spoon the sugar mixture over the top of the dried fruit.

5 Put the butter on the top so that it melts and oozes down as it cooks.

6 Wrap the apple in a double thickness of aluminum foil, twisting the ends to form an easy handle for gripping from the top.

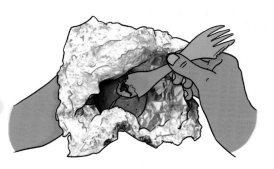

7 Ask an adult to help you place each apple on the hot coals of your campfire using long-handled tongs, Cook the apples for about 20 minutes, turning them regularly. An adult can test to see if they are cooked by pushing them with a gloved hand. They should be slightly soft. Leave them to cool for a few minutes before unwrapping them and spooning out the soft, sweet apple. Enjoy!

S'mores

These are an American campfire classic. And you know why they're called s'mores, right? Because no one can taste them without asking for "some more"! The only trouble is knowing when to say "no more."

Ingredients:

Cookies or crackers
Pieces of plain chocolate
Marshmallows

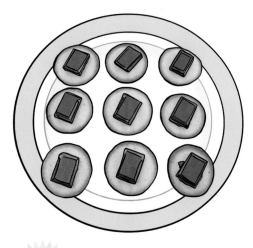

1 Put half the cookies or crackers on a large plate and top each one with a square of chocolate.

2 Thread two marshmallows onto a toasting fork or long stick and cook them over the campfire for a couple minutes, turning them all the time.

3 Let the marshmallows cool down just enough so you don't burn your fingers. Take them off the fork or stick and put them on top of a cookie or cracker (and its piece of chocolate) on the plate.

4 Use a second cookie or cracker to sandwich the chocolate and marshmallows together. Once the chocolate melts and the marshmallows have cooled a bit, you can tuck into the delicious gooey mess.

5 Make s'more!

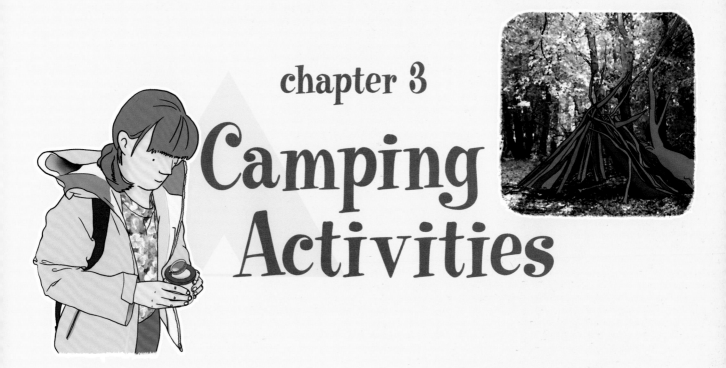

chapter 3
Camping Activities

Making a sundial

Why use a watch while you're camping when you can rely on nature to tell you everything you need to know? Try making your own sundial, all you need is a stick, some pebbles, a felt-tip pen, a watch (just to get you started; one with an alarm is best), and the sun, of course.

1 Start early in the morning on a sunny day, when you are planning to be around the campsite all day. Find a flat patch of short grass or bare ground with no plants growing on it and no trees blocking out the sun. Brush away any twigs, stones, or leaves.

2 Find a straight stick about 6 in. (15 cm) long, and push it into the dirt so that it stands upright on its own. You may need to soften the ground with some water first. Draw a circle in the dirt around the center stick.

3 You'll need a watch to set up the sundial on the first day of your camping trip, but once it's set up, you can put your watch away. Start as early as you can, and every hour, on the hour (i.e. when it is exactly 8 a.m., 9 a.m., etc.), place a pebble at the tip of the shadow cast by the stick. Using a felt-tip pen, write the hour on the pebble. Then set the timer on your watch for an hour's time, so you don't forget the next pebble.

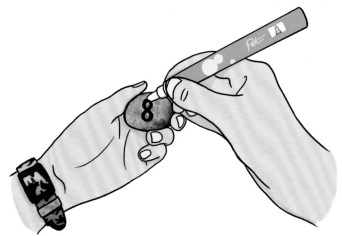

4 By the time the sun goes down, you'll have all the daylight hours marked out on your sundial. The following day you won't need a watch at all (provided it's not cloudy, of course!)

Treasure trails

Everyone loves searching for treasure, that is why a treasure trail is such a great game to play when you're camping out in the country. First you make a map, then you build twig arrows that you can leave along the trail. Finally, you need a prize for the trail winner. Just make sure your treasure-seekers don't sneak a peek while you prepare your trail. It must be a surprise.

You will need:

Notebook, pencil, and pen

Used teabag

Sheet of thick paper

String

Twigs, feathers, leaves, pine cones, and pebbles—enough for all the treasure seekers to collect

The prize

1 First, plan your treasure trail by making a map. Start the trail from a landmark near your campsite, such as a large tree. Draw the tree on your map.

2 Now choose the second landmark on your trail—this can be anything from a fence or a pile of logs to a picnic table or an old shed. Walk to your second landmark, counting your steps as you go. On your map, draw the second landmark and add an arrow pointing to it from the first landmark. Draw a dashed line between the two, with one dash for every step you counted.

3 Carry on drawing arrows and landmarks on your map, not forgetting to include a dash for every step between each landmark. You'll need about six or eight landmarks altogether for a proper treasure trail.

4 Now it's time to draw your real treasure map. Wet the teabag a little and wipe it all over the thick sheet of paper to make it look like an old map. If you tear the edges as well, it will really look like a pirate's map. Leave your map to dry.

5 Copy the treasure trail you made in your notebook onto the real map. Also write notes telling your treasure-seekers what to pick up at each landmark as they go along. You could say "Collect two black feathers from under the log," for example, or "Right here you will find a pine cone on top of oak leaves." The treasure-seekers must collect these little markers as they proceed along the trail.

6 Now collect a pile of sticks to make arrow signs with. You'll need two short sticks and one longer one for each arrow.

Tip

If you and your treasure-seekers are good at using a compass, you could include compass bearings on your map and the treasure-seekers would have to follow these instead of stick arrows. It would be good practice, as you would have to be very accurate!

7 Put the map, sticks, and markers plus your prize in a bag and set off to lay your treasure trail. Follow your map around and, when you reach a landmark, carefully place on it the marker you have described on the map. (Try not to make it too obvious—you need to challenge your treasure-seekers!) Then make an arrow with three sticks pointing in the direction of the next landmark. Once you reach the final landmark, hide the prize.

8 When everything on the treasure trail is ready, hand the map to your treasure-seekers and challenge them to find the treasure.

Pooh-stick racing

Invented by that famous bear, Winnie the Pooh, all this
game needs is a river and a footbridge. Be warned: it can
get very competitive!

1 Each player finds a straight
stick a few inches/centimeters
long, as well as some feathers
and leaves.

2 Using a long blade of grass (or a piece
of string), tie the leaves and feathers
around the end of your stick so that
you'll be able to spot it easily once it's
in the river.

3 Everyone stands on the footbridge, leaning over the railing and looking upstream, with the water flowing towards them. On the count of three, players throw their sticks straight down into the water. Make sure you all keep your feet on the ground and don't lean too far over the bridge.

4 Quickly turn round and look over the other side of the bridge, downstream. The winner is the player whose stick emerges first from under the bridge. Don't try to get your stick out of the river, as this could be very dangerous. Just make another one!

Cloud-spotting

Camping isn't all about bright, sunny days. If it gets really cloudy, why not try a bit of cloud-spotting? It's great fun. Here are 11 cloud formations you can look for.

Cumulus

The puffy, cotton-wool clouds you see either on their own or in groups.

Cumulonimbus

The very big, very tall clouds you see during thunderstorms.

Cirrocumulus

Small, white patchy clouds that form in rows high up in the sky.

Stratocumulus

Like cumulus clouds, but bigger and lumpier.

Altocumulus

Medium-size patchy clouds that form in rows and look like fish scales.

Stratus

The flat layers of cloud that sit low in the sky.

Cirrostratus

Hazy layers of cloud that sit high in the sky.

Altostratus

Sheets or layers of grey cloud.

Nimbostratus

Dark layers of cloud that seem to have no shape.

Cirrus

The thin, wispy clouds you see high up in the sky.

Contrails (vapor trails)

Okay, so they're man-made—by airplanes—but they're still clouds, aren't they?

Going for a hike

Once you've put up your tent and prepared your campsite, you'll want to explore the countryside around you. Ask the grown-ups if you can all go hiking.

You will need:

Map

Food and water

Compass

Good walking shoes or boots

Sunscreen and hat

Waterproof jacket

An extra layer of clothing in case it gets cold

First-aid kit

Backpack

Binoculars

Large stick

1 Using the map, plan a hike that takes in interesting natural features such as woodland, hills, and rivers. If you're going to be walking near private land, make sure you stick to legal paths.

2 Don't be too ambitious. Start off by hiking small distances—you can always go farther once you're used to it.

3 Build in some food stops during your hike, because a hungry hiker is a grumpy hiker. And remember to keep sipping water, especially if the weather is hot.

4 Just because you're walking along, it doesn't mean you can't play fun games with your fellow hikers. "I Spy" is a good one, since there will be lots to see. "Follow the Leader" is another great game: you all walk in a line, and whoever is at the front of the line (the leader) has to do funny movements as they walk along. Everyone else has to copy them. Take turns in being the leader.

5 Always keep an eye out for wildlife. As long as you don't make too much noise, you should come across lots of birds and even the odd mammal. Interesting insects, flowers, and plants are easy to spot. Sometimes you see tracks left by larger animals. A pair of binoculars will help you to see wildlife in the distance.

6 A hiker needs a good stick. Choose one that is strong but not too big. It should come up to your waist. A grown-up will help you to snap it to the right size.

How to use a compass

Hold the compass flat in front of you on the palm of your hand. After a few seconds, the needle will stop moving and point toward north. Turn the compass around so that the needle points at the letter N. Now you can work out which way you're facing, and which way you need to go. As you're walking along, regularly check your compass so that you don't veer off in the wrong direction. If you want to head in a particular direction, for example west, it's a good idea to choose a landmark (a tree or a large rock, for example) due west on the horizon, and head for that. Once you reach it, check your compass again and select a new landmark to head for.

7 Learn to read a map. Most countries sell special maps that are perfect for hiking. In the US there are USGS maps, in the UK there are Ordnance Survey maps, and in Canada there are NTS maps. Learn to pick out landmarks such as churches, footbridges, transmission towers (electricity pylons), and woods. Get used to reading contour lines, which tell you whether you're going to be walking up- or downhill. Remember: the closer together the contour lines, the steeper the hill.

Climbing trees safely

All kids enjoy climbing trees, but if you haven't had much practice, take care and perhaps ask a grown-up to help you. Remember that it is usually easier to climb up than to climb down, so don't go too high.

1 Find a big tree with lots of strong branches that will easily hold your weight. Make sure there are branches growing near the ground for you to start your climb. Don't choose a tree with rotten or dead branches.

2 First of all, you need to find a foothold. Then look for a branch above your head to hold onto.

3 Now climb up the tree, one branch at a time, switching between handholds and footholds. To be safe, it's important to keep three of your four limbs in contact with the tree at all times.

 4 Branches are strongest where they first grow out of the tree trunk. They are weaker if you stand on them farther away from the trunk. Avoid thin, weak branches—it's a long way down!

5 Always watch out for splinters. It's a good idea to climb trees wearing thin gloves.

 6 Always think about your route back down as you're climbing up. You don't want to end up like a cat— stuck up in your tree.

7 You don't need to climb very high to enjoy a great view of the countryside around you. See if you can spot your tent. Try keeping very still for a few minutes and watching and listening for birds and animals that live in the tree. Keep a tight hold on the branches while you're looking and listening.

8 Climb back down slowly and safely, switching between footholds and handholds, as you did on the way up. It's almost always best to climb down facing the tree trunk.

Animal-tracking

Most wild animals are very shy and because they can sniff us out, they often run away before we can get close enough to look at them properly. But they leave all sorts of things behind: tracks, feathers, fur, and of course, poop!

You will need:

....

Your camp diary and a pencil

Magnifying glass or bug pot

There are sure to be lots of animals near your campsite, but which species they are depends on which country and region you're in. Here are some clever tips on spotting their tracks.

1 Look for animal footprints in the soil. Wet soil is best because it leaves the clearest tracks. Try to guess whether the animal was a bird or a mammal. Birds normally have spiky footprints. Look closely and see if you can spot the outline of a mammal's hooves or claws. How many toes does the animal have? You could sketch clear footprints in your diary.

Deer   Robin   Fox

Wild boar   Rabbit

2 Look out for feathers or bits of fur. Birds can accidentally drop feathers anywhere. Mammals often leave fur outside their burrows, or when they pass through small gaps in a hedge or fence.

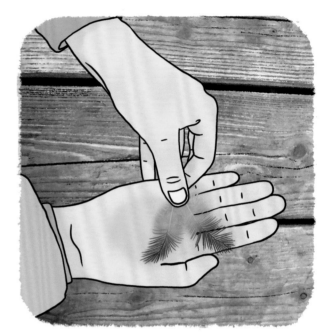

3 Like us, animals have to drink. They often leave tracks, feathers, or fur near ponds and streams.

4 Some animals love to bite and chew trees or pieces of wood. Often they are trying to get at the bugs living inside.

5 Can you spot any nuts or seeds that have been eaten by rodents? Animals eat on the move, and it's easy to spot the leftovers of their meals.

6 Male deer rub their antlers against trees, normally in late summer when they're trying to get rid of the velvet that covers them. Look out for the marks on tree trunks.

7 Some large mammals sleep out in the open. You can often see where their sleeping bodies have pressed down a patch of grass.

8 Animals are great builders. Look out for webs and cocoons made by spiders and insects. Try to find nests made by birds, bees, wasps, or ants (but never poke at them—you don't want to disturb whatever lives there, or get stung yourself). Notice the burrows made by mammals.

9 Look closely at the leaves on trees and bushes. Insects will often make small holes where they eat. Sometimes they consume whole leaves. When you find an interesting bug, use your magnifying glass or bug pot to see it better, but always put it back where you found it.

10 Slugs and snails may move really slowly, but they leave behind long, twisty trails of goo.

11 All animals do poops, and they're not very shy about where they do them. Serious animal trackers don't call it poop, though. They say "droppings" or "scat," instead. Hold your nose and look closely, and you may even see what the animal had for its last meal.

deer poop

fox poop

rabbit poop

Bird-spotting

There are thousands of different birds to be spotted, from tiny little cheepers to big, powerful birds of prey. It all depends on which country you're camping in. But wherever you are, there are some basic rules to help you enjoy watching our feathered friends. Remember to be patient, since birds can be very shy.

1 Try to take an experienced bird-spotter with you on your first outing. If you don't know one, make sure you take a bird-spotting guide book instead.

You will need:

Local bird-spotting guide (illustrations are often better than photos)

Dark clothing

Binoculars (small ones will do)

Your camp diary and pencil

2 Don't wear bright clothing. You need to blend into the background so you don't scare away the birds. And keep the noise down while you're spotting—walk stealthily and only whisper.

3 Hang your binoculars around your neck so they rest on your chest, ready for action.

5 Keep both your eyes and your ears peeled. Birdsong is really important in identifying a species. Some birds have a very distinctive song, but hide in the bushes when they're calling. You can learn a few of the sounds made by common birds in your area by listening to online recordings before you go on your outing. You can even get apps for a smartphone that can help you identify birdsong!

4 Start spotting in the morning, when birds are looking for their breakfast.

6 Feather color is important, but it's not everything. You should also notice the shape of the bird, its size, its markings, the way it stands or flies, and its behavior. Markings on the wings and tail are often very helpful for identification. Remember that birds replace their feathers throughout the year, so they may look different from the pictures in your book. Male and female birds of the same species can look totally different.

7 If you want to be very professional, you could make notes and sketches of the birds you see. Write down exactly where and when you spotted them, what they were doing, what the weather was like, and how many birds there were. More simply, you could just make a list of the birds you have spotted.

Key:

1 Crown
2 Wing
3 Tail
4 Flank
5 Breast
6 Bill

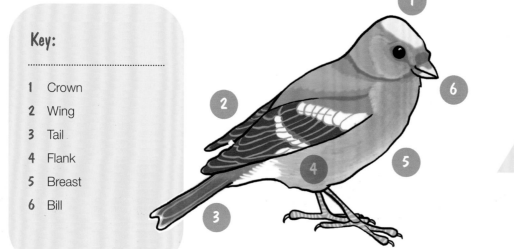

8 Learn the names of the different parts of a bird (see diagram).

9 If you're not having much luck, put some food out to lure the birds to an area near your tent. Sunflower seeds are popular with many species. Be patient and you'll soon have some hungry visitors.

10 Be kind to the birds. Don't get too close to nests or areas where the birds like to display.

Pond-dipping

There might be a pond or small, shallow stream somewhere near your campsite—and where there's water, there's always really amazing wildlife to be discovered.

You will need:

White plastic container (old ice-cream tubs are good)

Small fishing net

Teaspoon (a white plastic one is best)

Bug pot with magnifying lid, or a small white bowl and a magnifying glass

Identification chart or book

Your camp diary and a pencil

 1 Half-fill the plastic container with pond or stream water. It's good to use a white container because you'll see any animals best against a white background.

2 Find a safe position on the bank of the pond or stream and slowly sweep the net through the water. Creatures love to hide where there are lots of weeds. Try not to scrape the net along the bottom of a pond or you will scoop up lots of mud, which will stop you seeing what you have caught. If you are dipping in a very shallow stream, you could, with an adult's permission, paddle in it wearing rubber boots (wellies). Then try holding the net downstream of a big stone while you lift it. Alternatively, hold the net in front of you while you kick the gravel at the bottom of the stream.

 3 Bring out the net and return to the bank where you have left your plastic container. Put the net over the container and gently turn it inside out, so that everything you have caught falls into the water.

4 To take a closer look at the creatures you've caught, use the teaspoon to scoop them into the bug pot or small bowl. Then you can use your magnifying glass to examine them. Most will be tiny ones like nymphs and larvae, but sometimes, if you're lucky, you might find bigger beasties in there. Every pond or stream has predators in it with cool ways of attacking their prey.

5 Try to identify the creatures you have found. List them and make notes about them in your camp diary.

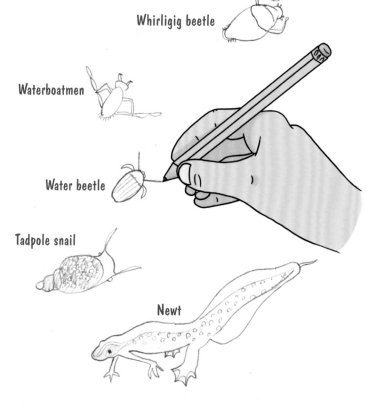

Whirligig beetle

Waterboatmen

Water beetle

Tadpole snail

Newt

6 Once you've had a good look at your catch, gently pour the water and creatures back into the pond or stream.

Sleeping-bag race

Sleeping bags aren't just for sleeping in. During the day you can have great fun racing in them, though remember that you will need your sleeping bag to keep you warm at night, so be careful not to tear it or get it wet. Perhaps it's best to save this activity for the last morning, before you pack up!

 1 Choose a flat stretch of dry ground that's clear of stones, thorns, and twigs.

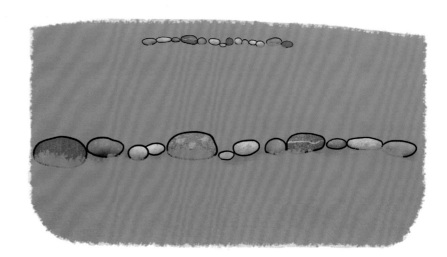

 2 In the dirt, mark out a start line and a finish line. If the ground is grassy, use a line of pebbles instead.

3 You should all line up on the start line, standing up inside your sleeping bags. Place your feet right at the bottom of the bag and use your hands to pull the bag right up to your chin.

4 Someone yells "Ready, steady, go!" and then you all jump as quickly as you can in your bags toward the finish line. You must stay inside your bag at all times.

5 Whoever crosses the line first has to lie on the ground in their sleeping bag. Everyone else then piles on top of them.

Making glass jar lanterns

Don't throw away your old food jars. Before you go on your camping trip, use them to make cute and colorful lanterns to light up your campsite.

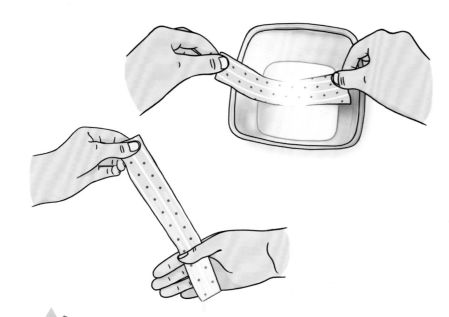

You will need:

Sharp scissors

Scraps of fabric

Craft (PVA) glue

Old, clean plastic container (such as an ice-cream tub)

Three old glass jars, cleaned and with the paper labels soaked off

About 3 yards (3 m) thin jewelry wire

Selection of beads and sequins

3 battery-operated tea lights

1 Cut the fabric into strips measuring about 1 x 8 in. (2.5 x 20 cm). Pour some glue into the plastic container and add a little water. Mix it up well so it's nice and runny, then dip the strips in to coat them with glue. As you take them out, run them between your thumb and finger to rub off any excess glue and then stick them onto the inside of the jars so that they make vertical stripes. Leave them to dry overnight.

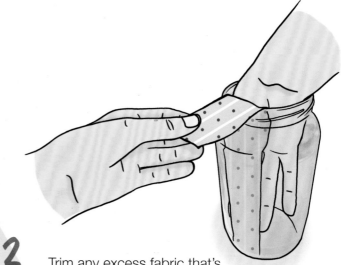

2 Trim any excess fabric that's sticking out around the neck of the jars.

 3 Cut a piece of wire long enough to fit around the neck of the first jar with a bit to spare. Wrap it around the neck of the jar and twist the ends together to secure it. Now cut a piece of wire long enough for the handle, with a bit to spare. Take one end of it and twist it around the neck wire several times. Now thread lots of beads and sequins onto it. When you have enough, twist the end firmly around the neck wire on the other side of the jar, making sure the beads and sequins don't slip off as you do this.

 **4** Place a battery-operated tea light in each jar. Don't use a real candle in case it sets fire to the fabric in the jar.

5 Hang the lanterns in the trees near your tent.

Shell pendants

If you're camping near the seaside, keep an eye out for shells with holes in them. They make great necklaces. Pebbles with holes in will also work. You can then decorate your necklaces with paint or colored pens.

You will need:

Flat shells or pebbles with holes in them

Assorted colored pens or paints

Metallic gold or silver pen

Thin string or wool

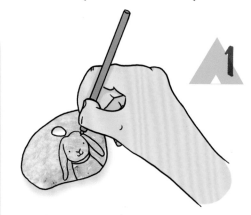

 1 Make sure the shells or pebbles are clean and dry, then paint or draw a design onto one of them. Any design will do, but make sure it's colorful and bold.

 2 Extra decoration with a metallic pen will add a bit of sparkle.

3 Cut a piece of string or wool long enough so that it goes easily over your head and with about 1½ inches (4 cm) extra for tying knots.

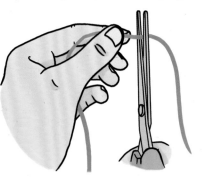

 4 Fold the thread in half. Poke the two loose ends through the hole in your shell or pebble, and back through the loop in the thread. Pull tightly to secure.

5 Thread on a couple of small shells with holes in them and tie them in place above the main pendant.

6 Finally, tie the two loose ends of the thread together so that the pendant hangs down over your chest.

Bowls made of bark

Old, peeled tree bark is perfect for painting on. When you're out walking near your campsite, keep your eyes open for pieces of bark that have fallen onto the ground. Check they are dry—if they're wet or rotten you won't be able to paint on them. You'll need a big curved piece of bark to make a bowl, but smaller pieces can make lovely decorations, too. Instead of brushes, use little sticks dipped in paint.

You will need:

Pencil

Pieces of bark

Small paintbrushes or sticks

Paint in various colors, including white

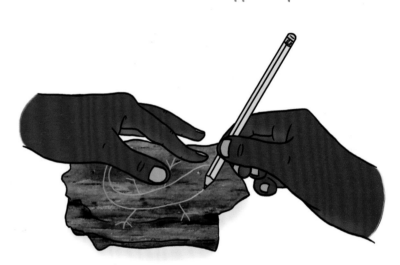

1 Using the pencil, draw the outline of the picture you want to paint onto the piece of bark. This lizard looks great—just like the pictures Australian Aborigines traditionally paint on their bark bowls.

2 Dip a small paintbrush or stick into the white paint, and apply dots to make a pattern around the outline of your picture.

3 Use dots with different shapes and widths to add other colors to your picture. Follow the lizard design, or make up your own.

Origami boat races

Origami is the traditional Japanese art of paper folding. Here you can learn how to make origami boats to race on a stream near your campsite. All you need is a sheet of paper about 6 in. (15 cm) square for each boat you want to make.

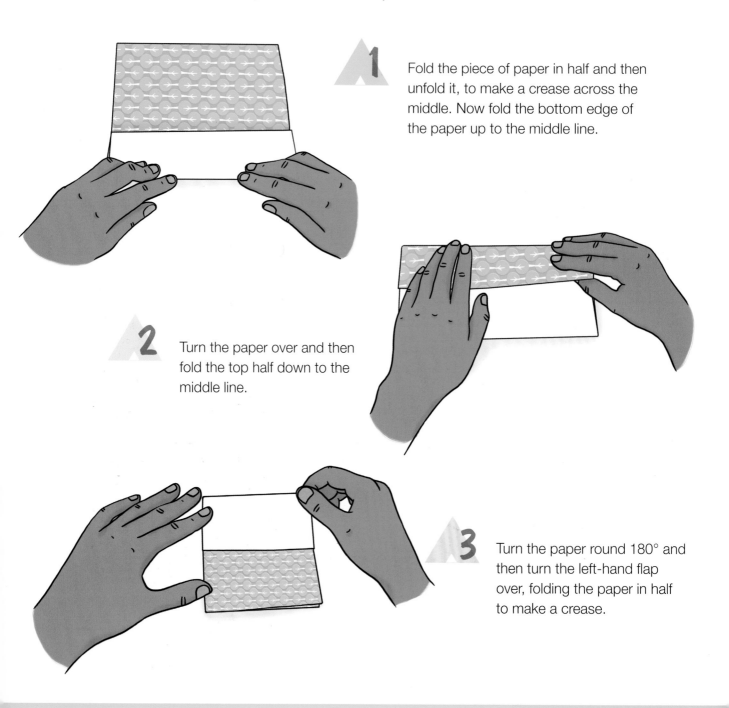

1 Fold the piece of paper in half and then unfold it, to make a crease across the middle. Now fold the bottom edge of the paper up to the middle line.

2 Turn the paper over and then fold the top half down to the middle line.

3 Turn the paper round 180° and then turn the left-hand flap over, folding the paper in half to make a crease.

4 Open out the paper and fold both edges in to the middle line.

5 Open out the top of the left-hand flap, flattening it into a triangle fold. Repeat on the right-hand side.

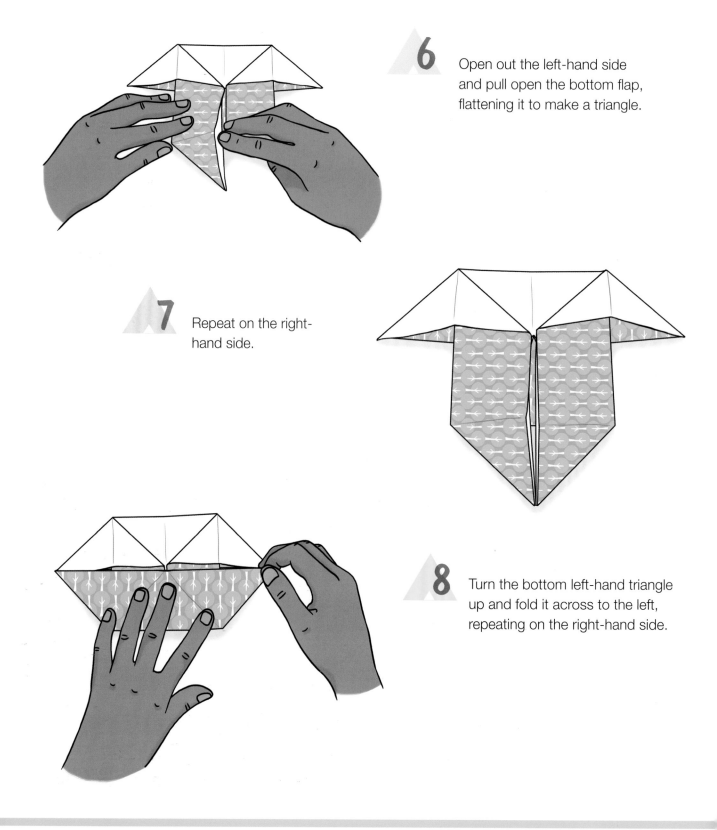

6 Open out the left-hand side and pull open the bottom flap, flattening it to make a triangle.

7 Repeat on the right-hand side.

8 Turn the bottom left-hand triangle up and fold it across to the left, repeating on the right-hand side.

9 Pull open the lower half of the boat and fold the top half down into the opening.

10 Finish by opening out the boat into its full shape.

11 Once you've made several origami boats you can race them on a shallow stream with your friends. Only race your boats in very shallow streams where it is safe to catch them. Don't let them get away to become litter!

Building a den

Wherever you're camping, there's sure to be a wood or forest nearby. You may even have pitched your tent in the middle of a forest. This is the perfect place to build a den—something all kids should learn to do.

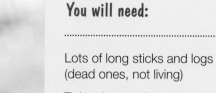

You will need:

Lots of long sticks and logs (dead ones, not living)

Twigs, leaves, ferns, and moss

Large piece of bark

Pen or charcoal

1 All dens need a frame. The best is a living tree with a low branch growing out sideways, a few feet off the ground. This will be your roof structure. It's best if the ground below your tree is flat, dry, and not too stony.

2 Collect lots of sticks. They need to be long enough to lean against the branch you have chosen, sticking out at an angle like a tent. Make sure you use only dead wood that has fallen from a tree. Don't rip off live branches.

3 Lean your largest sticks against the branchso that they form the shape of an upside-down "V." Then use thinner sticks to fill in the gaps between the larger sticks. The back of your den will be the main trunk of the tree, and the gap at the front of your den will form a doorway.

 4 Cover the frame of your den with lots of twigs, leaves, ferns, and moss. Make sure you fill all the holes and cracks. This will make your den warm and cozy.

5 Use more leaves, ferns, and moss to cover the floor of your den so that it's comfortable when you sit in it.

6 Last of all, you need to make a sign for your den so that passersby know it's occupied. Use a large piece of bark for this. Think up a name for your den and write it in pen or charcoal on the inside of the bark. You may want a second sign with "Grown-ups keep out!" on it. A den should always be a grown-up-free zone!

Making a teepee

Alternatively, you could build a teepee, by leaning your branches into a central point.

1 Find a stick with a "V'" shape at the top. Then secure two other "V" topped sticks to the first, the idea is to create a sort of tripod, by interlacing the "V"s together.

2 From there, you can lay other sticks on top of this structure, spacing them evenly, leaving a hole at the front for your doorway.

3 Use your foot to scrape the needles and leaves from the ground around your teepee to the outside edges. This provides a windbreak for the outside of the teepee and it also means that any insects won't feel comfortable crossing the yard you've now cleared around your den, so no creepy-crawlies in your bed!

4 Fill in any gaps with shorter sticks, then cover with moss and ferns, making sure there are as few gaps as possible. Line the floor of your shelter with moss and ferns to make it comfortable.

5 Always leave the forest or wooded area how you found it, so make sure you take your teepee apart before you go.

When the Sun Goes Down

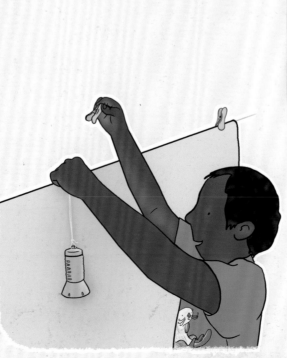

Scary ghost stories

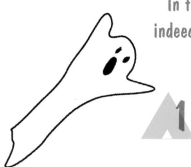

In the pitch dark, late at night, camping can be very spooky indeed. To make it even spookier, what about telling some ghost stories? Here are some great tips.

 1 Before you go on your camping trip, download ghost stories from the internet and print them out. There are lots of websites where you can do this for free. Ghost stories are even more scary if you tell them, rather than read them out, so read a few through first and remember what happens (you don't need to learn them off by heart).

2 Wait until after supper, when darkness has fallen and everyone is ready to hit the hay.

3 Make sure everyone has turned off their cellphones (mobile phones). There's nothing scary about electronic beeps.

4 Use a flashlight (torch) to light up your face while you tell your tale. It will make you look really spooky. If everyone else turns off their flashlights, they will concentrate on watching and listening to you.

5 Pretend that you don't actually want to tell your ghost story. If you sound reluctant, people will think you're scared, too. That makes it all seem more real.

6 Change the details of your ghost story to make it sound local and very recent. So, even if the original story was set in London or New York City, change it to the nearest town to your campsite. Claim that it happened just a few weeks ago. This will trick people into thinking it all happened for real.

7 Bring your surroundings into your story. If you're camping by a river or next to a mountain, then make the scene of the haunting that spot. If it's a foggy night at your campsite, then make it foggy in your story.

8 It's important to act nervous while you tell your story. People will get really scared if you keep glancing around you into the darkness, or if you're jittery and jumpy.

9 End your story with a sudden fright. You could shout out the final line of your tale unexpectedly to give everyone a shock. Or you could suddenly grab the arm of the person sitting next to you.

10 If you really want to scare someone, choose a victim in advance and ask a friend to sit next to that victim while you tell your story. Just as you come to the sudden fright at the end, your friend should reach behind the victim's back and grasp their shoulder. They will jump clean out of their skin!

Moth-catchers

There are over 160,000 different types of moth around the world, many more than butterflies. A great way to get a close look at them is by building a simple moth-catcher.

You will need:

String

Clothes pins (pegs)

White sheet

Two good flashlights (torches)

Cardboard box

Scissors

Lots of empty egg cartons

Sticky tape

Stapler

 1 Tie a length of string between two trees and, using the clothes pins, peg the sheet to the string so that it hangs down to the ground.

2 Tie string around one of the flashlights and hang it behind the sheet.

3 Open up all the flaps on the cardboard box. Cut off the two smaller flaps. Cut four thin strips of card off the short end of one flap.

4 Pull the lids off the egg cartons. Use the sticky tape to stick an egg carton inside each wall of the cardboard box. Place the other egg cartons on the floor of the cardboard box. The moths will settle inside these egg cartons.

 5 Using the stapler, clip two of the thin strips that you cut up earlier flat against the inside of each end of the cardboard box. Staple them at an angle and then push the remaining flaps under them so that the flaps point downward. Now there will be a narrow slit between the two flaps for the moths to fly into.

6 Put the second flashlight inside the box so that it points upward (head flashlights are good for this because they don't fall over), and place the box in front of the sheet. Once it gets dark, switch both flashlights on and leave your moth-catcher for an hour or so.

7 Return to the moth-catcher and count how many different types you have caught. You'll be surprised at how many there are. Always let them go afterward.

Shadow puppets in your tent

Camping trips are so exciting that it's not always easy to go straight to sleep when you go to bed, especially when you are camping with friends. If you are lying in bed, not feeling sleepy, you can use your flashlight (torch) to make amazing shadow puppets on the walls of the tent. One person holds up the flashlight, while the other makes animal shapes using their hands. Make the shadow bigger by bringing the flashlight closer to your hands and smaller again by moving it backward. You could make up stories with some of these different characters.

Crab

Move your hands sideways so it looks as though your crab is scuttling sideways.

Cockatoo

Move the thumb on your right hand and he will look as though he's eating.

Crocodile

Make his jaws snap shut.

Dog

If you move your thumbs your dog will twitch his ears. Move the fingers making his mouth, and add barking sounds.

Goose

Move your fingers to make your goose peck.

Horse

If you move your hands up and down it will look as though the horse is galloping.

Kangaroo

Make him jump like a real kangaroo.

Rabbit

Wiggle your rabbit's ears and make him use his paws to scratch his nose.

Snail

Wiggle your fingers to move your snail's antennae.

Snake

Pluck two long pieces of grass for your snake's fangs and hold them between your fingers.

Tortoise

Wiggle your fingers to make his head move.

Buck

Use your fingers to create this deer's dramatic antlers.

Woodpecker

Move your hands back and forth so it looks as though your woodpecker is pecking a tree.

Wolf

Tilt your hands up so it looks as though the wolf is howling at the moon.

Stargazing

Trillions of stars and so little time! It can take a whole lifetime to become an expert in stargazing, but just a few minutes to spot some of the more interesting constellations (groups of stars). And a camping trip—out in the countryside, with your heads poking out of the tent—is the perfect occasion. Remember, though, that the stars you can see change as the Earth spins. So the constellations in winter can be different from those you see in summer.

What you need:

A telescope isn't essential, but binoculars will give you that extra bit of vision. (But don't ever look at the sun through binoculars, as this will damage your eyes.)

The moon

No, of course it's not a star, but our nearest neighbor is a very interesting rock all the same. The best time to view it is not at the time of a full moon, but when it's between being a new moon and a full moon. Using your binoculars, try to spot the craters (caused by meteorite impacts) and its biggest seas. They are called seas because ages ago people thought they were filled with water. Look for the Sea of Serenity, the Sea of Tranquility, the Sea of Fecundity, the Sea of Crises, and the Sea of Clouds.

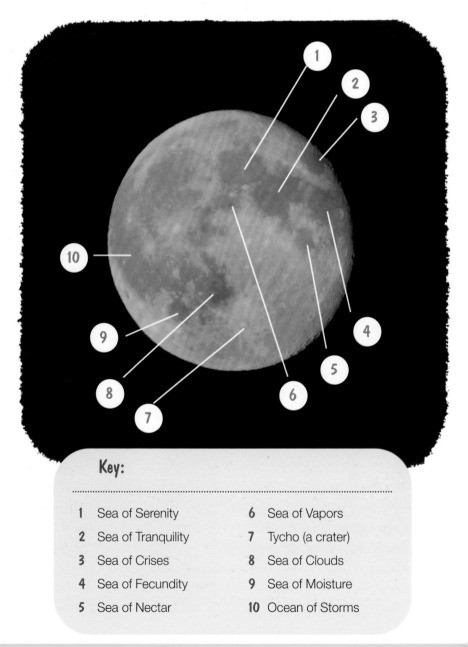

Key:

1	Sea of Serenity	6	Sea of Vapors
2	Sea of Tranquility	7	Tycho (a crater)
3	Sea of Crises	8	Sea of Clouds
4	Sea of Fecundity	9	Sea of Moisture
5	Sea of Nectar	10	Ocean of Storms

Shooting stars

You can spend hours looking for a shooting star, and then with just one blink you miss it. But on some nights you can be really lucky and spot a whole meteor shower. Remember to make a wish if you see a shooting star.

Constellations

Depending on where you are in the world and what time of year it is, you will spot different constellations in the night sky. Here are some of the most famous ones. Remember that different countries give different names to the constellations.

Orion

The seven brightest stars of Orion make the shape of an hourglass, with Orion's belt cinched across the middle. This constellation is best seen during winter in the northern hemisphere and summer in the southern hemisphere.

Big Dipper (the Plough)

The Big Dipper is made up of seven stars in the shape of a pan with a long handle. You can spot it during most of the year in the northern hemisphere. If you draw an imaginary line upward from the front of the pan you will find the North Star.

North Star (Polaris or the Pole Star)

Every other star seems to rotate around Polaris. That's because it lies directly above the North Pole. Visible all year round in the northern hemisphere, it's actually a cluster of stars.

Mars

This one's not a star, of course—it's our next-door planet. It's easy to identify, appearing pale red in color. Unlike stars, planets don't twinkle.

Southern Cross (Crux)

Small and shaped like a cross, this constellation is visible in the southern hemisphere pretty much all year round.

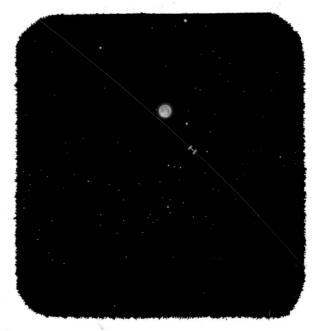

Satellites

If it moves slowly across the sky and doesn't blink, then it's most likely a satellite high up in the Earth's atmosphere. (Or a UFO!) There are thousands up there, although many of them are just space junk. The International Space Station is one of the easiest to spot.

The Milky Way

The galaxy our planet is in is called the Milky Way. It looks like a creamy band of stars spread across the night sky.

Index

Useful organizations

US

American Hiking Society: www.americanhiking.org

Camping equipment: www.usoutdoor.com; www.campmor.com

Dangerous animal advice: www.animaldanger.com

Maps: www.usgs.gov

North America Camping Club: www.northamericacampingclub.com

UK

The Camping and Caravanning Club: www.campingandcaravanningclub.co.uk

Camping equipment: www.decathlon.co.uk; www.millets.co.uk

Maps: www.ordnancesurvey.co.uk

Ramblers: www.ramblers.org.uk

Acknowledgments

PROJECT MAKERS

Charlotte Liddle & Lucy Hopping: pp 82—83

Clare Youngs: pp 84—85, 86—87

Mari Ono: pp 88—91

RECIPES

Louise Pickford: pp 36—37, 38—39, 40—41, 44—45

Heather Cameron: pp 42—43

PHOTOGRAPHY

Claire Richardson: pp 6, 83, 85, 87

Ian Wallace: pp 29, 36, 38, 44

Carolyn Barber: p 89